101 Piano Practice Tips

How to get your kids to the keyboard!

By Tracy Capps Selle

Dedication

I'd like to say a special "thank you" to my wonderful parents! Thank you for loving me unconditionally and for giving me the gift of music. I'm truly grateful for all those piano lessons!

To my sweet husband, Kevin. I love sharing life with you-what an adventure! Thank you for always loving and supporting me. I can't wait for the next 20 years with you!

And to my son, Matthew. I love being your mom! Thanks for teaching me to be a "*Marvel*ous" mom and for making me smile. Every. Single. Day. You make me want to be a better person.

Finally, I'm grateful to God for loving me and opening my eyes to the truth of His Word.

Romans 15:13

Copyright 2013, revised in 2015

Table of Contents

Introduction	4
The Top Ten Things You Can Do Right Now	8
Create a Great Environment	14
Make a Practice Plan	18
Attitude is Everything	24
How to Encourage More Practice	26
How to Encourage Good Quality Practice	30
Make it Fun—Accountability	38
Find Opportunities for Your Child to Perform	44
How to Help Older Students	48
All Practice Does Not Need to be at the Piano	54
Things to Remember	60
Tips from Kids	62
Tips from Parents	66
Help! My Child Wants to Quit Piano Lessons!	68

101 Piano Practice Tips

Introduction

Most kids don't want to practice the piano. And let's face it. In today's world, there certainly are a lot of distractions. iPads. iPhones. Video games.

Practicing the piano is usually the last thing a child wants to do.

So where does that leave parents? Most are frustrated. No parent wants to nag all the time, but what choice is there? And since piano lessons are expensive, when kids don't practice, many parents simply give up.

A lack of practice is also frustrating for piano teachers. It's nearly impossible to teach new concepts when students aren't putting in the practice time.

In the end, it all adds up to a vicious cycle and kids suffer the most. When children don't practice, it's harder to advance. Then they get discouraged.

Many end up thinking that they aren't good at playing the piano when in reality, they just didn't put in the practice time.

The good news is that there is a solution. In this book,

I share all the tips I've discovered during my 14 years of teaching piano. You'll learn fun, practical ways to get your kids to the keyboard—without nagging.

But this book goes one step further. You'll also discover some simple ways you can help them have better *quality* practice. Even if you've never had a music lesson in your life!

Here's what one parent, Cindy Wood, writes about these ideas:

"Tracy makes practicing fun, yet challenges kids at the same time. I have 4 children, ages 6-14, and they are all at different levels in piano and mindset. The tips are practical, easy to apply, I have already put them to use and getting GREAT success."

Mark Paulson, a New Jersey piano teacher and composer, writes:

"It's practical advice for motivating students to practice. There are games and apps that can stimulate practice. There are performance suggestions and even ways to encourage students who might be considering quitting their lessons. This book also provides suggestions for the necessary length of practice, and ways to address situations when a student is involved

in numerous activities."

The tips and tricks you're about to read have been proven to get results. Read through the tips and choose a few to try out. Think about what would appeal to *your* child.

The tips are divided into sections and some of them will work in different seasons of your child's life. When your kids are older—or you need a change of pace—come back to this book for some fresh ideas.

For now, just select a few tips and keep an eye out for what seems to work best.

I promise if you follow through with the ideas presented in this book, you'll see your child *choosing* to practice the piano. The *quality* of their practice will improve. It won't be long before their teacher notices and your child will see the difference too!

In the end, your child's learning will soar through the roof and you'll breathe a sigh of relief because you didn't let them quit.

Don't be the kind of parent who simply waits on the sidelines until their child *wants* to practice. Odds are —it'll never happen. And piano lessons are too expensive for you to let another "no-practice" day go by.

This is your chance to help your child have good quality practice, discover a love of music, and make success a reality—all while having fun at the same time.

The Top Ten Things You Can Do Right Now

1. Make practice a priority! Your kids won't learn to play the piano unless they actually spend time playing the piano.

When children don't practice, they don't play well and then they start to believe that they can't learn to play the piano. The truth is simply that they didn't put in the practice time!

You're paying a lot of money for lessons, but success won't happen unless your kids practice several days each week.

It sounds obvious, but many parents forget this basic concept. Get those kids to the keyboard!

2. Have your children practice right after their lesson and the very next day. Their practice will be much more effective because everything they learned is fresh in their minds.

This is one of the very best ways to ensure good *quality* practice.

3. Before your children begin to practice a song, have them look the piece over. Teachers will often mark tricky rhythms or easily missed notes.

If your kids start by glancing over the piece and taking note of any teacher marks—before playing—they'll be much more likely to pay attention to those sections when they begin to practice.

This is a simple concept that often takes less than a minute, but can really make a big difference. Most kids won't do this unless their parents remind them.

4. Consistency is key. Consistent practice of 4-5 days a week is better than 1 or 2 days of longer practice. A short, focused 15-minute session will do wonders for your children!

Some very young kids may only be able to do 10 minutes, but if they're consistent with that 10 minutes every day, their learning will soar!

Even children with the busiest of schedules can find just 10 minutes a day to practice.

5. Should you remind your children to practice? YES! Don't hesitate to remind them. Children wouldn't brush their teeth if we didn't tell them to. It's the same with piano practice.

In this book, you'll find lots of obvious ways to remind your children and some more subtle ways so you don't feel like you're constantly nagging them.

6. After your children have practiced their assignments for the week, encourage them to go back and play a few of their old favorite songs.

This is a great way to keep their skills fresh. Plus, it's fun!

The more they play, the better they'll get and then they'll want to play even more. It's a win-win situation.

7. Be a cheerleader! Let your kids overhear you telling someone how well they're doing. Be specific and sincere.

Don't say they're great at practicing the piano if they rarely do it. Instead, you could say you're amazed at how quickly they learn *when* they practice.

The idea is to find *something* to compliment!

8. Do your children a favor and encourage them to play in front of people when they're beginners. If they start performing early, they won't get as nervous at recitals later.

This doesn't have to be a big deal. Even just a phone call to grandma during practice would work. A Skype call would be even better!

Remember, being able to perform or talk in front of people is an important skill and this is your chance to give your children a head start!

9. Let your kids see you practicing something or learning a new hobby. Children often think that skills magically appear. Or people are born with amazing abilities.

As adults, we know that every expert was a beginner at some point.

You can help your children learn this truth early in life if they see you working to develop a new skill.

10. Decide on a minimum number of years your

children will commit to piano lessons. Some kids learn very quickly in the beginning, but when they start to feel challenged, they want to stop.

Don't let them quit! Every child struggles at some point—and that's good! It means they're growing and learning.

When I began playing the piano, my 2 best friends started taking lessons at the same time. After 2 years of playing, we all wanted to quit—and my friends actually did. But my parents wouldn't let me stop because we had already decided that I would play for a minimum of 3 years.

Today I'm so thankful they made me stick with that decision. They gave me the gift of music and that's exactly what you're doing for your kids. It's such a blessing!

101 Piano Practice Tips

Create a Great Environment

11. Give your children a practice place designed just for them. Most parents tend to decorate for themselves, but your piano practice area should be full of things *your kids* love.

For example, instead of having several family photos or knick-knacks on top of your piano, display a cute collection of stuffed animals or dolls. Whatever would make your child smile.

If you have little boys, your piano might end up covered with plastic lizards—but that's okay!

If you have teens, cover the piano with pictures of them and their friends. Another idea? Display their favorite book series or maybe a photo of their favorite singer. This could really inspire them!

Whatever you decide, just remember that this space should be designed with your children in mind so they'll be happy to sit down and practice.

12. Have a special "practice hat" that can only be worn when your children are playing the piano.

I have one student who got wolf ears from Great Wolf Lodge and wearing those turned into a happy tradition. She wore those ears everywhere—even to her piano lessons week after week, for months on end!

You could also use a sparkly tiara or a Spiderman costume.

Get creative and think about what *your children* would enjoy. Be silly and make it fun!

One warning: Keep an eye on them. If practice time turns into playtime, they should lose those privileges for a while.

13. If you have young children taking piano lessons, let them take a favorite stuffed animal to sit on the piano or in nearby chair.

I have a couple of students who really enjoy doing this and it's a way for me to get them to focus better. "Rufus wants to hear you play this song one more time, but a little faster!"

Some teachers may frown on this, but if your child stays focused and doesn't turn it into playtime, I bet most would be willing to try it.

14. If at all possible get a real piano, known as an acoustic piano. Why?

First, it gives your children a better experience. For example, when children use a keyboard, they often have trouble finding middle C.

Second, some keyboards don't have a pedal and your child will be using one sooner than you think!

Another reason to get an acoustic piano is because piano keys have a very different touch from keyboards. On an acoustic piano, striking a key harder will produce a loud sound; a lighter touch will make a softer sound. There are some keyboards that address this issue.

Finally, kids simply get a confidence boost when they play on a "real" piano. Imagine hitting the golf course with a set of toy golf clubs—it would never work! Your child needs a good instrument to learn properly.

Talk with your teacher and visit a music store to see the options. If you shop around, I bet you can find a piano at a good price. I had one student whose church was selling a couple of older pianos and they got a great one for $300.

If finances are a problem, full-sized keyboards are still a good option, but discuss it with your teacher. Some have very strict rules about what instrument students play on.

The bottom line? If you're going to invest in piano lessons, your kids deserve to practice on a good instrument.

Make a Practice Plan

15. Decide *how often* your children should practice. Each teacher has certain practice requirements, but most teachers require practice about 4-5 days a week. Find out what your teacher recommends.

16. Next, you need to decide how much *time* your kids will spend practicing. For example, you could set a goal to practice 100 minutes each week.

If your child is a young beginner, their practice may literally take just 5-10 minutes each day. Their weekly goal would need to be much lower.

17. Once you know the weekly practice goal, you can come up with a plan. Perhaps your children could practice 20 minutes, 4 days a week. Or maybe 15 minutes, 5 days a week.

Have your kids help!

Remember, there's no wrong way to do this. Just set a goal and give your children some direction. Plus, they'll be much more likely to follow through if they helped create the practice schedule.

18. When you make your plan, keep in mind your children's energy level. Do they focus better earlier in the day?

Many parents of younger students say that their kids do best if they practice in the morning *before* school starts.

Warning: this probably won't work with teenagers!

19. What if your family prefers flexibility? No problem! Practice times don't have to be scheduled.

The important thing is that your children are making time to practice the piano each week.

Determine right now that you'll make it a priority.

20. Here are a few reminder ideas:

Grab an index card, write the days of the week on it and have your children circle the days they practice.

Put a Post-It note on their bedroom door, reminding

them to practice. You could even stick the note to the TV: "No television until you've practiced your piano!"

Another option? Many kids have iPods or phones now. Have them set an alarm as a reminder.

Think outside the box and figure out a way to remind your kids.

21. You might want to try having your children use a timer. If you look around, you can find a bunch of cute timer apps that could help make practice more fun.

For example, "See if you can play this song 3 times before the timer runs out."

Be careful though. Using timers can be stressful for some children. Or they might race through the songs and make a lot of mistakes.

Pay attention to your kids and see what works for them.

22. Track your children's progress. Most kids love charts and calendars. Get creative; use a jazzy font.

Add glitter or superhero stickers and mark off the days your child practices.

When piano lesson day comes, it's very encouraging for kids to look back over the week and see their hard work.

If you have an older child, you could just use a basic practice calendar and put them in charge. Or use an app.

There's a free version of Music Journal that's pretty good at tracking practice time and I'm sure there are many others.

Whatever method you decide, know that giving your teens responsibility for this will teach them to be more organized and responsible with other areas of their life.

You can find Music Journal at www.axe-monkey.com/musicjournal/

23. This might surprise you, but don't require practice every day.

Most people only do hobbies or activities a few days each week. I love to crochet, but I don't do it every day.

Encourage 4 days of practice and 3 days off. Your children will be happier and that'll make you feel great.

If your kids want to play more—fantastic! But it shouldn't be a daily requirement. It's just not necessary to schedule practice time every day.

24. Help your children set small goals that are easily achieved.

Maybe you have a teen who's only practicing once a week, but you'd like for him to practice 4 times a week. Start with a goal of twice a week.

Once that becomes a habit, add in more days—gradually!

You could do the same if you're tracking minutes. Set a small goal and build on it.

It's very encouraging to set a goal and actually reach it.

101 Piano Practice Tips

Attitude is Everything

25. Some students get upset when they make mistakes. I get it. Everyone wants to do things right the first time.

Explain to your children that learning something new means mistakes will happen—and that's okay!

Let's face it, if your kids already knew how to play the piano, they wouldn't be taking lessons.

26. Keep a running list of your children's favorite songs to play. Have them choose a favorite song to kick off their piano practice. This is a great way to start, especially if they're not in the mood to play the piano that day.

The Plucky Pianista, Melody Payne, has a cute printable that you can download for free. (thepluckypianista.blogspot.com)

Using that same list, encourage your children to run through the songs once a week so they don't forget how to play their favorites.

You'd be surprised how many students "forget" how to play old songs. Reviewing them occasionally keeps the songs fresh, gives your child a sense of accomplishment, and provides a fantastic review!

27. Fix your children a little snack before practice, especially if they're practicing right after school. A little pick-me-up is usually needed and will help your child focus better.

28. Keep an eye on the big picture. Yes, you want your children to learn to play the piano, but many other life-skills are being developed.

Your children are learning goal-setting, discipline, responsibility, and patience—all while learning to play an instrument.

None of these skills come quickly, but if you stay upbeat, happy, and gently encourage, your children will succeed.

How to Encourage *More* Practice

29. Rewards! All children are different, so spend some time thinking up a good reward designed with *your* kids in mind.

Perhaps you could offer a coupon to get out of a chore in exchange for an extra day of practice. Would your children like to earn more electronics time or maybe a sleepover with a friend?

Believe it or not, I have one student who will memorize just about anything for a can of chicken noodle soup! Another student really likes cats, so occasionally I'll reward her with a coupon to play with our cats for 10 minutes.

The reward possibilities are endless and you could always ask your children for ideas too!

30. Anticipation can be a lot of fun. Try buying a special prize for your children. Wrap it up in fancy paper and have it sitting in a visible spot somewhere in your house.

The trick is that your kids can only open it when they reach a practice goal that you've set.

31. Have you ever recorded your children playing the piano? Kids love this and it's so easy to do these days. Try it and let them enjoy the music.

Often, beginners are so focused on the notes that they fail to hear the music.

I bet they'll be excited to hear how great they sound, which in turn, will encourage more practice.

32. You might want to implement a "practice before electronics" rule or require practice before your kids head outside to play.

One word of caution: if you think your children will rush through their practice unfocused, it's better to use a different system. You don't want their practice quality to suffer.

(More on this in the next section.)

33. Connect your children's practice with another activity that's done every day.

For example, maybe your children could practice right after breakfast. There was a season when my son would always practice *before* doing his math homework because it was a way to put off his least favorite subject.

Be willing to try a few things and see what works for your family.

34. Who said rewards are just for kids? Why not reward YOURSELF if you get your children to practice, say 12 times a month. That's only 3 practices a week—a very reasonable goal. Your reward could be a manicure or a Starbucks latte.

Find whatever motivates YOU to get your kids to practice. It's a win-win!

How to Encourage *Good Quality* Practice

35. Encourage your children to play new songs slowly. Many kids play so quickly that they lose the rhythm and make mistakes.

(Sometimes they actually "practice in" those mistakes and then learn the piece incorrectly.)

After your kids have practiced a few days and really learned the song, they'll find it much easier to pick up the tempo.

36. If your children have a particularly difficult song, encourage them to play their hands separately at first.

Once they know what each hand is supposed to do, putting them together is much easier.

This can also simply boost their confidence a little!

37. If your children are making too many mistakes and getting frustrated, they're probably playing too fast or they could just be tired.

Have them take a break and try again later.

Minimizing any frustration will certainly help with the quality of practice.

38. For very young children, 5 minutes of daily practice might be enough.

Many children physically cannot handle a longer practice time—and that's okay!

Have them work up to a couple of 5-minute practices each day and they'll develop the skills necessary to handle a longer time.

Consistency is much more important than practicing for a certain length of time.

See what your teacher thinks is realistic for your kids.

39. Daily practice—or at least most days—really does make a difference.

The more your children practice, the faster they'll improve and this will help them enjoy piano a lot more.

40. Encourage your children to *focus* when they practice. Some kids are in such a rush to finish, they play incorrectly.

Many will breeze right past mistakes, never even bothering to go back and try again.

A short, focused practice is much better than a longer one with no concentration.

41. Encourage your children to write on their music.

You don't want your kids to write down every note name, but if there are a few sections they mess up every time, marking those spots will help.

Sometimes I'll even just put a star or sticker beside tricky spots.

The idea is to give students a "heads up" to remember something we talked about.

42. Get the right teacher. The best way to do this is to think about your goals.

Yes, you want your children to learn to play the

piano, but are you secretly hoping to raise a composer or a concert pianist?

Do you want your kids to participate in theory competitions or play in the praise band at church one day?

Many parents simply want their children to develop a love of music and enjoy playing the piano when they're adults.

There's no wrong answer here, but if you decide what's right for your family, you can find the right teacher.

One warning here: once the basics of piano are taught and your children have a strong foundation, they should be playing music they enjoy.

I had one student transfer to me from another teacher. The parent was discouraged because the girl was never practicing and I was the "last chance" before they would stop lessons completely.

I found out later that this girl's former teacher did nothing but teach classical music and she only taught the child about 2 lines of a song each week!

This adorable little girl was bored to tears! She had played the piano for several years, but had only been taught classical music, which she was sick of playing.

What did I do?

I taught her other genres of music. Ragtime, Blues, and oh how she loved playing Christmas music.

In no time, we turned her attitude around and she was playing the piano with joy. It was such a blessing to see!

Of course, all kids will have to play songs that aren't necessarily fun—that's part of the learning process.

Nonetheless, children should definitely be playing music they enjoy. That's really the best way to get them to the piano consistently.

Having the right teacher is a big part of the solution.

43. Encourage your children to count out loud.

Most teachers will tell students when they should do this, but typically students ignore that advice because they feel silly.

Counting out loud is a wonderful way to master tricky rhythm. Even if your child only whispers, it'll work wonders!

44. Ask questions! If your kids don't understand something, talk with the teacher and see if there's something you can do to help. It might be a quick fix or it could be a concept that just needs a little time.

Either way, teachers will most likely have some great suggestions and are usually thrilled when parents are willing to help.

45. Some kids enjoy a game called "Penny Practice." Simply put 3 or 4 pennies on the left side of the piano. If your kids play a difficult section correctly, they move a penny to the right side of the piano.

If they play it again and miss a note or rhythm, then any pennies on the right must be put back to the left.

The goal is to play the section correctly three times in a row and move all the pennies over. And yes, they get to keep the pennies!

One hint: this works even better if you use quarters or Hershey's Candy Kisses, especially if you have teens!

46. It's important for kids to learn to read notes on

the staff.

Encourage beginning students to keep their eyes on the music as much as possible—even if they've memorized the piece.

Every time they play the piano and look at the notes, they're doing note review. This will enable them to play more difficult songs sooner and they'll love this.

Memorization will come later.

47. Remind your children to fix mistakes—not just repeat them. When kids mindlessly practice without correcting mistakes, it makes it nearly impossible to fix them later.

Encourage your children to circle the tricky notes or rhythm and then play that section slowly.

With a little time and patience, they'll probably be able to fix the problem and move ahead faster.

48. If you have several children taking piano lessons, take the time to assess their attitude toward each other. Do they encourage each other? If so, fantastic—count your blessings!

Often, siblings will turn piano lessons into a competition and that's not good.

If kids go into their practice thinking their brother or sister plays better than they do, they'll have a defeated attitude and won't succeed. Also, the confident sibling could get arrogant and not work as hard.

Here are some things you can do to alleviate the situation.

First, don't compare your children; point out whatever each child is doing right.

Second, ask your teacher to consider putting them in different books. Many teachers do this automatically because they understand the issues with siblings.

Finally, try to have your kids practice as separately as possible. Maybe one child goes to the piano, while the other heads to his room to listen to the radio.

Do whatever it takes to make sure your children aren't feeling discouraged.

Make it Fun: Accountability

49. Find another family who has children taking piano lessons. Perhaps the kids can be "Piano Buddies."

They could set practice goals and celebrate together when they succeed in completing the goals.

Maybe they could talk on the phone or even email each other whenever a pep-talk is needed.

50. Grandparents can be great encouragers!

If you have grandparents who live far away, have your kids call them on the phone and have a little concert right over the telephone!

I have one student who loves to Skype with her grandmother. It's a blessing to everyone!

The idea is simply to find anyone who will support your children and encourage them to practice the piano regularly.

When I was just 13 years old, I became the pianist of my church. The organist at the time was a wonderful, older woman who met with me weekly to practice together. We had such fun!

Not only did her encouragement help me grow as a pianist, she and her husband became like adopted grandparents to me.

Taking the time to find someone, besides yourself, to encourage your children will really pay off.

51. Do your children have friends who play the piano? If so, maybe they could play a duet. It's always fun to play with a friend!

Even if the kids have different teachers, I bet the teachers would work on their parts separately and you could get the kids together when they're ready to put the song together.

Playing with another person is a great skill to learn and this would provide a wonderful opportunity to try it.

52. Speaking of duets, if you have a couple of children taking piano lessons, ask them if they'd like to work on a duet.

Yes, this could be tough for some siblings, as I

mentioned earlier. Many do argue a lot and playing together could backfire, but I still think it's a good idea to try. After all, they can always stop if playing a duet turns stressful.

I find that many siblings have fun playing together and often break out in giggles!

53. Encourage your children to host a little recital for family and/or friends.

I have one young student who has her family wear "recital hats" and they all sit around the piano while she performs.

What a fun way to encourage more practice!

54. Have a goal. It could be a mini-concert for friends, or how about a "Piano Party" at your house? You could invite several friends over who play the piano and they could all take turns performing.

Maybe you could host a "Music Party" and invite kids who play *any* instrument. Have the kids bring their flute, sax—whatever instrument they play and let everyone have the chance to perform.

One tip: make sure you follow up the performance

with some yummy treats!

55. What are *you* working to accomplish? Do you play an instrument? When was the last time you sat down to practice?

Of course, your gift might not be playing music, but don't use that as an excuse.

Let your child see you working on *something*—anything! Crochet an afghan. Finish a woodworking project. Try a new recipe. Exercise a little more!

Make a pact with your children that if you all accomplish your goals, then everyone gets to go out for frozen yogurt.

56. Make sure your children know exactly what is expected of them each week.

All assignments should be written in some type of notebook. Clarify with the teacher if necessary.

Your children also need to know how much practice you expect of them.

Understanding expectations will save a lot of

frustration in the long run.

57. Find a role model. Do you know of any older children who play the piano? Or maybe a musician at church? Perhaps one would be willing to encourage your child.

You may want to talk with your teacher. It's possible that she has an advanced student who could act as a "mentor" for your child.

This is something that would benefit both students!

Find Opportunities for Your Child to Perform

I mentioned in my "Top Ten Tips" that's it's important to encourage your children to play the piano in front of others.

Your goal is for your kids feel comfortable in front of people, so don't force them to perform. Just gently encourage and motivate—with rewards if necessary!

Again, remember the hope is that your children will learn to enjoy sharing their talents, without pressure and without stress.

It's much better to inspire than require. With that in mind, here are some ideas that might appeal to your children:

58. If a neighbor drops by your house, encourage your children to play a song or two for them.

59. One of my students has a friend who plays the piano and sometimes they have what they call a "Piano War."

They see who can play the most songs from memory. Or sometimes, they compete to see who can play the fastest.

Not only do these girls have a blast, it's a great way for them to get self-motivated. As a bonus—they're getting comfortable playing the piano in front of others!

It might work for your kids, too.

60. Do your children love stuffed animals? Teddy bear concerts are fun! You could line up the animals on the chairs, couch, table—the more animals, the better.

Try to think of what theme would appeal to your children. Maybe a jungle or circus theme? Perhaps your little girl has a doll collection? I bet they would make a fabulous audience.

Think of what would inspire *your child* to play music!

61. Your children should learn to play "Happy Birthday." Let them play it whenever someone has a birthday.

There are many easy versions online and this is a fun way to encourage your kids to play the piano in front of others.

If there's a piano in your children's Sunday school class, talk with the teacher. Maybe your kids could play the piano for everyone's birthday?

This might work at school as well if your child is in choir or band and there's a piano around.

If you have friends and/or family who live in another city, your child could play "Happy Birthday" for them over the phone or using Skype.

62. Many churches (and schools) sometimes have break-out activities for kids. If there's a piano around, see if your children might want to play a song. I have one 6th grade boy who enjoys playing hymns during the offering.

Some kids might not like the "pressure" of performing routinely, but this student just really enjoys it.

His parents have definitely succeeded in helping him discover his love of music early in life.

63. Is there a nursing home near you? Most have a piano and the residents love to be entertained! Call and see if you can take your children (and maybe a couple of friends) to perform for the residents.

Go out for ice cream afterward! Make it a monthly event!

64. I hope your piano teacher has a recital. If so, make sure your children participate.

And don't leave once your children have finished. Hearing others play the piano—especially the advanced students—will inspire your kids.

One day, hopefully *your kids* will be the advanced students inspiring others.

How to Help Older Students

65. Teens don't like to be micro-managed and yet they they often need it! If your children are older, it might be time to work on transferring practice responsibility.

A good way to accomplish this is to be "hands off" and still give them some subtle reminders.

One idea is to take an index card and write the days of the week on it. Tell them that they need to practice 4 days that week and have them mark off the days when they practice.

It's their responsibility to remember and turn the card in to you at the end of the week.

Make sure you put the card in a place where your kids will see it every day. Maybe their desk, or tape it on the mirror in the bathroom.

If they do this for a month or so with success, reward them! Most teens love gift cards, like iTunes or Google Play.

66. Make sure your children play songs they enjoy. This is so important as kids enter the teen years.

If your teacher focuses on classical, but your child prefers ragtime, you should have a talk with your teacher.

All kids need to learn fundamentals, but once a student has a basic foundation, they should be working on at least a few songs they truly enjoy.

67. You don't have to rely on your teacher to find music. Many composers now deliver their music digitally and several of them are a hit with teenagers.

You can listen to most every song online and even look at part of the sheet music. Compositions are all available for immediate download and most cost less than $3.00.

Your children might be able to learn the songs on their own, or they can have their teacher help them. Every teenager in my studio loves the following composers:

Jennifer Eklund is always a favorite. You can find her at PianoPronto.com She offers a variety of genres and every song is a hit with kids. You just can't go wrong with her music.

Another favorite is Daniel McFarlane. You can listen

to his work and instantly download his compositions at SupersonicsPiano.com Most of his work tends to be fast and furious. Boys love it!

If you have children who enjoy blues and jazz, then you must check out Elena Cobb at ElenaCobb.com She lives in England and is another fantastic composer. If you find a song you like on her website, you'll see a "Shop in the USA Amazon" button. Click there to easily make purchases. Higgledy Piggledy Jazz is always a favorite with my students.

68. If you have older kids who've been playing the piano for a while, their songs are probably getting much longer. Sometimes mastering them can be overwhelming.

Encourage your teen to break the song down into sections. Once a small section is mastered, then combine a couple of sections until the entire song is complete.

This could take several days, or longer depending on the length of the song, but in the long run it's a great way to learn faster!

69. Get a metronome. This can be great for kids who

need help feeling every beat.

Have your children start the metronome at a lower speed than is necessary for the song. Slowly increase the tempo until they are able to play the piece at the desired speed.

Your children's teacher should be able to help you get started with this.

In the next section, I'll give you the names of several metronome apps that are fun to use.

70. Encourage your teens to focus on one task at a time. It's hard to work on notes, rhythm, tempo, and dynamics all at once. Remind them to start slowly and be patient.

71. Make sure your children don't move ahead in their book. I know it can be tempting, and it may seem like your kids benefit from it, but moving ahead without instruction can backfire.

When children jump ahead and learn something incorrectly, it can be very frustrating for both the teacher and the student.

If your kids are self-motivated and really want to move ahead—talk with your teacher.

Sometimes I give kids a "challenge" piece to learn. We'll look at the piece together, I'll point out any tricky spots, and then they get to work on it at home. This works great for some kids.

72. Songs don't have to be practiced from start to finish. Many students find their songs are relatively easy to play except for a couple of tricky parts.

What do most kids do? They play the heck out of the easy sections, stumble through the hard parts, and just keep on going.

Unfortunately, the tougher sections never get better without a little extra work.

To fix this problem, encourage your kids to find the difficult passage in the song and work on that *first*.

Once that part is mastered, it's a lot easier to move on with the whole song.

This is a fantastic way to grow as a pianist, but children rarely do it unless their parents remind them often.

101 Piano Practice Tips

All Practice Does Not Need to be at the Piano

73. If you want your children to learn to play the piano, of course they need to actually play the piano. But truthfully, all practice does NOT have to be at the piano.

In fact, your kids could work on learning to read music while you're driving them to soccer practice! There are lots of online games and apps that focus on reading music.

It's a great way to have your children work on learning their notes or rhythm, while having fun at the same time. For more experienced students, this can be a great review.

One note: Remember, apps and websites are wonderful educational tools, but as I mentioned earlier, they shouldn't replace practice time at the piano. Think of these ideas as just another way to give your children a love of music. It's all learning!

The next few resources are some favorites in my studio. Keep in mind that new apps are coming out all the time, but this list will get you started.

74. Two of my favorite apps for learning to read notes are Treble Cat and Bass Cat.

Unfortunately, they're rather expensive, costing about $5.00 each, but they're great apps and kids enjoy them. Both are perfect for beginners, since they start teaching at middle C.

This would also be a good review for older students. Most students need a little extra practice with the bass clef, so Bass Cat would be great to brush up on those skills.

One note: I've seen both of these apps go on sale, so you might want to watch for that.

75. Another cute app is NoteWorks. It has an adorable little monster who gobbles up the notes when you get them correct.

There's a free version for beginners that works quite well. The full version costs about $5.00.

76. Flashnote Derby is another fun app that costs only .99 and is great for working on note-naming.

You have a racehorse and if you get enough notes correct, your horse wins.

This app is very kid-friendly and is a favorite in my studio.

77. If you have young children, I highly recommend The Most Addicting Sheep Game. It's a fun way to help kids hear the beat of the music and at .99, it's totally worth it.

One warning: the name is accurate—it really is addictive! And the tune is super catchy.

78. Another free app that's helpful with note naming is My Note Games. There's a free version and it's a great way for kids to brush up on their theory.

79. Worksheets are another good way for kids to learn. There are lots of fun, free (or inexpensive) music worksheets you can find online. Why not get some for your kids?

If you have a musical background, you could easily check their work. If you can't correct their work, talk with your piano teacher.

I'm sure any teacher would be thrilled to have a student do a little extra work. (And you might win the Parent of the Year Award!)

The Plucky Pianista (Melody Payne) also has a lot of games and worksheets. She offers printables that review note identification, intervals, major and minor keys, composers and more! You name it, she's got it!

Melody's very artistic, so the themes are adorable and appropriate for both boys and girls. As an added bonus, most of her work is $2.00 or less.

Visit her website and get some fun worksheets. You'll also find lots of freebies. Use Selle10 for a 10% discount on any purchase!

(teacherspayteachers.com/Store/Melody-Payne and thepluckypianista.blogspot.com/p/printables.html)

The website Fun and Learn Music also has great worksheets. And yes, they're free.

80. If you want to expose your children to great composers, Classics for Kids is an excellent website to visit.

Kids can learn about composers and also play several

online games. We used this quite a bit when my son was younger.

81. If you're looking for a metronome app, you'll find lots to choose from and many are free. Download a couple and play with them. See which your kids prefer.

I like Tempo, by Frozen Ape. Steinway Metronome is another good app that's free and easy to use.

101 Piano Practice Tips

Things to Remember

82. Be patient. Everyone progresses at their own rate, so don't compare your children to other kids—especially a sibling!

Every day that your kids practice, they're getting better. That's what really matters.

83. Remember that you're not just helping your children learn to play the piano. Many life skills are taught through music lessons—responsibility, determination, persistence, patience.

You're teaching your kids to set goals and accomplish them. Keep your eye on the big picture!

84. Be a good example! If you play a musical instrument, let your children see you practicing. Even just a few minutes here and there will inspire your kids.

I have one dad who loves playing classical music on the piano. His kids hear him playing often and it sets a great example for his family.

Is it time for you to dust off those old skills?

Tips from Kids

85. "I write myself a note and leave it to see in the morning. Sometimes I practice before school, but leaving a note always reminds me."

Bethany, 5th grade

86. "Do the fun songs first. That way you're happier when you work on the hard ones."

Lydia, 4th grade

87. "If you have a tricky song, try to make it into a game. Count how many mistakes you make and try to make fewer mistakes each time you play it."

Austin, 6th grade

88. "When I'm having trouble with a song, I'll go to the page before and review. It helps sometimes!

If I'm really frustrated, I'll play an old favorite and then go back to the hard song later."

Lauren, 6th grade

89. "I just really love piano. If I have a song that I don't like, I try to remember that if I practice it, then I can move on to better songs sooner."

Anna, 5th grade

90. "I try to not worry about recitals. I just remember that I'm only 12 years old. I'm not a professional!"

Lauren, 7th grade

91. "You have to practice because you want to know the notes better."

Brodey, Kindergarten

92. "Playing duets with my sister is fun because I'm not by myself.

We also do silly things, like play the piano with our toes!"

Halima, 6th grade

93. "Whenever I don't want to practice, I start with a song that I know really well and like."

Matthew, 7th grade

101 Piano Practice Tips

Tips from Parents

94. "I guess my practice tip would be to encourage every practice session, whether it be 5 minutes or 50! Every moment they practice is a step in the right direction."

DeeDee, mother of a 5th grader

95. "My daughter practices the same day as the lesson and then practices at the same time each day to make it a habit. She loves to play."

Jamie, mother of a 4th grader

96. "I'm not sure she would be as dedicated if she didn't have such an amazing teacher. She enjoys playing the piano and she loves to make her teacher proud!"

Jessica, mother of a 2nd grader

97. "Austin enjoys playing, but finding a time when he is home and his dad isn't on the phone can be tricky. We have him practice in the morning after the younger boys and I leave for school since he has nearly an hour before he leaves. Works great!"

Donna, mother of a 6th grader

Help! My Child Wants to Quit Piano Lessons!

Honestly, this will probably happen at some point and it's usually for one of three reasons:

- Life is too busy.

- Your child is bored.

- Your child might think that piano is becoming too difficult.

The good news is that all of these issues can be overcome!

First, you need to talk with your kids and figure out *why* they're not enjoying piano lessons. Often, children aren't able to verbalize the problem because they don't know.

This is where you need to play the detective.

Has their schedule gotten more hectic? Do they not like the songs they're playing?

Maybe the songs seem really difficult and your children are getting frustrated?

If you can name the problem, you'll have a much better chance of figuring it out.

And truthfully, there could be several problems, but pick one to start with and work from there.

98. Let's say your children don't have time to practice and want to quit.

This often happens during the teen years when school gets more challenging and kids get busy in other activities.

The most obvious way to address this is to cut back on the number of activities your children are doing.

But truthfully, this rarely happens—kids don't want to be left out of anything and parents usually like to keep their kids busy.

This is where you simply have to decide your priorities. Is piano a priority?

99. During the teen years, I've found the best way to deal with busy schedules is to cut back to fewer practice songs each week.

Simply talk with your teacher and explain that your children's schedule is full, but you still want them to keep taking piano lessons.

See if your teacher will back off to just one or two songs each week.

Busy kids are usually thrilled to have only one song to learn.

Parents are happy because the kids are still committed to learning the piano.

Teachers are happy because the students are finding time to practice and are still moving forward.

It's a win-win situation for everyone!

100. Let's say your children are bored. What's the fun in practicing songs they don't like? I get it.

Make sure your kids are playing music they enjoy.

Of course, fundamentals need to be taught and won't always be fun, but I'm sure your teacher would be willing to find a genre that interests your children.

Especially if she realizes that your kids may stop taking lessons.

Any teacher should be happy to find music your children enjoy playing, but if she (or he) isn't willing to, then you would probably be happier with a different teacher.

101. Eventually, piano lessons just get harder.

New concepts are taught and your children may not grasp them right away. It can be frustrating if your children have always been fast learners.

When this happens, see if your teacher will take a step back and let your kids play easier music for a few weeks.

I've found kids are more successful if they just get a little victory. They're playing songs successfully again. Hurray! Life is good.

It's best if your children don't know about this. No one needs to tell them that the music is easier—they probably know and truthfully, they don't care!

They're just happy to be playing songs well.

In a few weeks—or months—the level can be ramped back up. The goal at this point is to simply help them find joy in playing the piano again.

102. Bonus tip: Stick with it.

Some weeks might be rough, but don't give up. Your kids will thank you one day.

Thank you for reading this book and for helping your children find their love of music.

You are the parent that every piano teacher dreams of having in their studio!

One last thing...

Please leave a review on Amazon if you enjoyed this book and it helped you in any way. It only takes a minute and I would appreciate it so much.

Please visit Amazon and search for 101 Piano Practice Tips.

Thank you!

Made in the USA
Lexington, KY
12 July 2016